Trumping
"Denial Don"

A
Poetic
Satirical Political Chronicle:
27 months
of the "Liar-in-Chief"
and all his "Best People"

Bill F. Writze

Dedication

This work is dedicated to all those whom have had their intelligence assaulted, sense of fair play violated, and belief in truth and honorable discourse trampled.

A special thank you to parents, grandparents, teachers, mentors, civic and religious leaders, and others whom have instilled in us a high standard for personal responsibility and conduct. As well, thank you to those whom have given us the ability to understand and push back against intolerance, indifference, deceit, and hateful behavior.

Special kudos to all those that have finally stood up and called this man out for who he is, since I did in my first collection of poems, "Trumping 'Believe Me.'"

Equally so, a pox on the houses of all those who chose to embrace, nay suckle, on his ample teats, and put self and party, above country. You will one day wish that Mudd or Arnold was your surname.

Introduction

These 130± poems were created as an continuation of my original collection (Trumping "Believe Me" 2016), which was a personal cathartic exercise. Only after sharing them with close friends did I realize they helped others cope with the angst of the Republican candidate, and now President.

These poems were written over a 27-month period from just after the Presidential Election to mid-February 2019.

In addition to the main villain, I have written on the troupe of bad actors rounding out his administration. The poems are presented in approximate chronological order to add continuity to the reader's experience.

There are a handful of rhyming 'schemes' employed, and the formatting has been deliberate to help the reader establish and maintain the rhyme.

The limerick style is used and can be identified easily by its five-line verse; they have a wonderful rhythmic style.

Hopefully, in some small way this continues to be a prescriptive for regaining your mental health, and a tonic for your soul. Recommended for all moral Democrats, Republicans, and Independents!

Author's Note

I'll simply say that any guarded optimism I strained to muster following his election, had the half-life of a popsicle in hell. Enjoy the critique!

Bill F. Writze   July 4th, 2019

Tronald Dump is Nucking Futs

There're no bugs in Trump's Tower, they're all in his head
Where logic and reason, have been pronounced dead

Again off the deep end, with his Twitter feed
To Breitbart born fantasies, power he'll cede

He lacks self control, this habitual liar
Only alt-right advisors, to him, inspire

When he talks about nukes, he's so cavalier
As self-image comes first, just his voice he'll hear

This king has no clothes, it's so plain to see
While serving the interests, of the, GOP

Republicans manage, to just look away
Ryan and McConnell, on you this stain, will stay

If party before country, is what you believe
The voters will note that, your seats, they'll retrieve

How long can good people, feign their contentment
Until they invoke, the 25th amendment

Election Day +10

It's been 10 days, since Trump prevailed
He begins to learn, what the job entails

He's met with Obama, called him, " A good man."
States, he'll seek his "consul", in the future again

Then it's time for appointments, and to choose nominees
And it seems that his picks, don't put most at ease

Of course he is draining, the swamp as he said
By giving them jobs, these reddest of *red*

Alt-Right and fringe players, will help run it all
So far they're all white men, most despicable

And what of Trump's kids, and his son-in-law
Nepotism, is one more, judgment flaw

Demonstrations and protests, still running strong
Tens of thousands in number, I'd say that's a throng

So where's the diversity, of gender and race
So far it's just sycophants, who crowd this space

Now Cruz and Romney, have been Trumped
As pundits and analysts, seem quite stumped

The honeymoon's over, as insiders move in
Will Trump will get handled, by masters of spin

Is he built for the bandwidth, that the job requires
Can't choose the workload, nor succeed by his *fires*

He can't sue to win, or claim Chapter 13
He won't play well with others, uses "i" to spell team

He's on the right track, for where we feared he'd be
It went south so fast, it's a hot mess, bigly

Red and Blue, and Trumped All Over

If you bleed red or blue, does it sound good to you
As 45, still, does offend

Now let's see if "The Donald," gets "Mitch McConnell'd"
With Ryan as Speaker, again

It seems none is clear, why Trump instills fear
As he acts, first as foe, then as friend

Will time soon reveal, just what is his deal
Dooming democracy, to it's end

So far his ways, show he thinks, in a haze
By every which Tweet, he does send

Pakistanis say cheese, Taiwanese feeling pleased
Will China and India, break or bend

There's only one Trump, who'll make us his chump
Presidential, in his world, of pretend

TRUMP'S END STINKS

Trump will be,, a cautionary tale
On his path, to becoming, an epic fail

By employing those, he has just crushed
Shows lack of preparedness, not being rushed

Perhaps he believes, once beaten, he owns them
Most likely, they'll run things, as he plans to phone-in

His victims, survivors, they'll stay in the game
Will they plot revenge, with deceit and no shame

But maybe he plans, to replace them tout de suite
With allegiances few, to him most are meat

He won't honor pledges, may not even try
Congress won't fund him, even though he's *their* guy

So he'll pass the buck, blame others as losers
Then turn on his Veep, the once leader of Hoosiers

Still Pence will tell him, how Congress is run
Ryan and McConnell, will show him, their fun

Then Trump will nickname them, as his ego must
Then this troubled presidency, becomes a bust

Yet wait, he's a scrapper, when there's something for him
He'll cry foul, not knocked out, thin skinned with strong chin

He won't be embarrassed, his biggest concern
He'll go all third-grade, with names he will spurn

Next he'll make a bargain, offer carrot or stick
Though he's well out numbered, and makes most people sick

He came in through the side door, and that's how he'll leave
As he buries himself, few will be bereaved

DELUSION CONCLUSION

Delusional Trump, would make us his chump
If we'd just believe, what he'd say
He can't tell the truth, he's no biblical Ruth
On that field, he'd love us to play

His ego writes checks, he says, "what the heck"
Up to now, it's worked out okay
So he doubles down, like a unknowing clown
As his fantasies, soon start to fray

Yet we get him now, to his lies do not bow
In time, he will just fade away
Know time will abate, his legacy of hate
And normalcy, may come back to stay

Appointment with Disaster

Rex for state, it's all now clear
Sadly though, it's my worst fear

We all thought Trump, would bury his foes
But as it turns out, that's not how it goes

The pattern is there, yet we don't think like him
Sit back and relax, and now I'll fill you in

We all know his skin, is as thin as it gets
And when he's not liked, he won't stop with regrets

So look at all those, that at one time, opposed him
He needs them to like him, and revere him, as chosen

Carson, Christie, and Cruz ate their words
Rubio and Romney's, transformation absurd

But they're appetizers, before the main meal
He needs the big winners, to endorse each deal

True captains of industry, and large heads of state
And every detractor, affecting his fate

Being *The Man*, demands lots of hard work
With his lack of knowledge, soon himself, he'll irk

So let's hope his ego, doesn't get what's required
And from frustration, to himself says, "You're Fired!"

SAME TRUMP, DIFFERENT CAMPAIGN

Today I heard, Trump reveal
He'd have run a different campaign
And in that moment, I did feel
He acknowledged his wrongs and their pain

But two seconds later, came the qualifier
If the "popular vote", was his goal
Then points out, Hillary got it wrong
You just can't fill, this narcissist's hole

At first he bragged, of the people's mandate
And we all know, that's not close to true
Especially with Clinton's, three million vote lead
As he knows, she's more popular too

That caught in his craw, so he makes up a lie
That the margin, was all from dead voters
What's wrong with this man, and the stories he plies
Addict talk, comes from this teetotaler

Though he proclaimed, an electoral landslide
But it's close to the bottom, of rankings*
His win, 46th of the 58 races
Not "The Greatest", more like, a spanking

* Trumps electoral college margin was ranked 46th from the top, of 58
presidential election results.

Climate Denier, Sky on Fire,
Bad Water Down the Drain
Oklahoma, Koch brothers, Tea Party
Birther Lovers, win a CIA-EPA Gain

Melania stays in New York, to do what Trump wives do
Raising kids without him, and hope decency, shines through

Might it be that Ivanka, becomes our saving grace
Make her First Lady, the White House's, female face

She brought Gore to Trump Tower, to talk climate change
Something no one near Trump, considered to arrange

She shares with us this earth, great motivation
Let's hope Dad responds, without hesitation

The EPA's new man, oh no, a denier
What's more, fossil fuel guy, will set the sky on fire

They'll promote coal, and drill more oil, of this we are sure
Caring nothing for our health, they'll move to places pure

Goodbye to water you can drink, as fracking does pollute
De-regulation de rigueur, as congress comes up mute

How do the Kochs quench their thirst, where does their water
come from
Perhaps Fiji™ or Evian™, or arctic ice unfrozen

Their Oklahoma congressman, will head the C.I.A.
And OK AG, will end the E.P.A.

"How much access have they bought," the average guy might say
People quip, "Don't be naive," it's all just, "Pay to play"

So what about the working man, and draining out the swamp
It seems Trump's done the opposite, obscuring it with pomp

His cabinet, a rich crowd, in Generals, and by wealth
Standing for the middle class, or those reflecting self

Is it over, are we screwed, we've done this by our voting
Holding Trump's feet to the fire, might lessen our foreboding

COURAGE, DUTY, CONSCIENCE

Dear Electoral College, please now acknowledge
The state of affairs, of today

Our last *balance and check*, so let's not wreck
This place where we work, play, and pray

In regard to your purpose, help, and not hurt us
Knowing what Founding Fathers did say

And the Republic save, against forces so grave
Show your courage, and duty display

With mere days till this reckoning, the country now beckoning
As our nation risks going astray

Come nineteenth of December, act well, don't surrender
And to your, own conscience, obey

Can You See the Pattern

Today Trump announced, on the Ides of December
There be no disclosure, as promised, he'd tender

No it's not déjà vu, we've been here before
With tax and health records, the first in store

And where are Melania's, visas and permits
They've never see daylight, like so many hermits

And what of the statements, against all the ladies
Whom he groped *down-under*, this paragon of Hades

That too was forthcoming, but never appeared
A lie, or forgetful, it's both we should fear

So again, here we are, with nothing to see
At least this time lacking his, "believe me"

So what will he do, with his assets and business
Nonsensical answers, give us tinnitus

Bipartisan consensus, "just sell it all"
But it's not like him, to avoid profit's call

He'll argue the President, is exempt and able
Then claim prosecution, is off the table

Then shrug when you mention, the Emoluments Clause
Then move on with conviction, and nary a pause

He'll bully and push, and claim highest ground
So don't try and reason, as many have found

The courtroom, his only, Achilles heel
Where judges aren't threatened, and truth's not surreal

Sometime soon his court, will be the Senate
Impeached for laws broken, when he claims, "just bent it!"

DON'T LET HOPE, MAKE YOU A DOPE

This cat has his spots, and it's said, they can't change
But when spin is applied, those spots rearrange

Now post election, he tells Leslie Stahl
"Don't worry protesters", based on nothing at all

What of "lock her up", his rallying cry
"I don't want to hurt them", but in her case, he try

He changes his stance, to what you'll believe
His core stands behind, fulfilling his need

The most ardent think, he lies to the rest
He's yet to do anything, we'll wait for a test

Delusion of Greater Grandeur

Our Emperor-Elect, wears no clothes
And of his faithful, no one yet knows

He got to the top, by hook and crook
By using, every, trick in the book

It's not to say, without DNC's help
Russia and Wikileaks, took part in this whelp

Still he's convinced, he thinks it's all him
His winning margins, less fat, and more thin

Lies and deception, are no big deal
Trump University, should so reveal

Slogans are vague, they mean what you wish
Get's facts from the web, then dirt he'll dish

He's qualified by, a TV show
For many voters, that's all they know

I think we're all confident, he thrives on attention
Each rally delights him, like a mini-convention

He should feel empowered, and ready to go
But having not crushed it, he feels somewhat low

He has a reality, of his own invention
It's based on delusion, and lots of pretension

And those that know better, they won't say a thing
As they'll be rewarded, when his praises, they sing

He relishes conflict, but he must prevail
Else he'll crush you with lawsuits, or threaten jail

It's an age old story, with no special twist
If you don't succumb, you're on his shit-list

BANKERS AND BILLIONAIRES

These billionaires'
Special interests we fear
Trump did not, drain the swamp
Topped it off, so clear

And this latest round finds
With each new nominee
They're all lobbyists
So how good, can this be

The country has talent
Most are not insiders
But he fears legitimate
So we get more liars

INAUGURATION PARTY OF TWO

The time is near for inauguration
And with it, a star-studded, celebration
So request your tickets, without hesitation
Their talent, an underage girl

The Rockettes were listed, to entertain
The ladies that balked, need not remain
If few do agree, that would be lame
This chorus line, won't kick and whirl

They tried the A-list, but none would have it
The B-list too, where most said, "jam it"
Mormon Tabernacle, played their gambit
The Marine Band, will get the referral

I know red states, have great talent too
How about Oklahoma, nominees total two
And what about Kanye, he seems to like you
Just the offer, makes showbiz folks hurl

So invite attendees, from your last rally
And to them opine, speech fit for an alley
Their talent, *applause*, in the thousands they tally
While "plorables", recall your each pearl

So why can't this president, find talent to muster
It feels, "Little Big Horn", reminiscent of Custer
Perhaps born of lying, and his vulgar bluster
Away from this, he'll try and *squirrel*

New Deals Sealed

No new deals, except Indonesia
Just another case, of Trump's amnesia

As Carl Icahn, assumes some new role
Freeport Mac mines, their monstrous hole

Of course Carl is, their largest shareholder
A conflict supreme, could these guys be bolder

New York Times, then Trump, outs Ethics vote
Him for timing, them principle, I'll note

Then he claims false credit, for Ford's decision
No new plant cross border, they downsized a division

Always boasting, lying, or adding to conflict
Know he'll never yield, till his title is "convict"

We've now less than three weeks, until he's sworn in
Kiss reality goodbye, and watch madness begin

USING COMMON CENSUS

If your party is Democrat, they've not served you well
They've gotten their ass kicked, as if you can't tell

Go back to the midterms, of 2010
Where Dems, lost House races, again and again

It seems all the "Hope", of 2008
Garnered less love, and a measure of hate

And then came the census, as with every decade
As Republicans drooled, with plans they've laid

They're betting their gridlock, would displace Obama
His populist issues, caused their donors trauma

For all of their scheming, they got it so wrong
As a second term followed, Hussein eight years strong

Without the White House, Red Congress did swell
As did State Houses, could the Dems not tell

Clearly through, gerry-man-dering
Republicans rigged, the whole voting thing

Illegal, perhaps not, immoral, certainly
Not representative, of the Land of the Free

They played the long game, and did us no service
The Peoples Work blocked, making us furious

As congressional maps, now favor their whim
A Democrat's vote, is diminished and slim

Now Trump taking power, and talking four more
A combo of words, make Dem's ears so sore

With DNC damaged, and trust in them shaken
They'll need the next midterm, for the faithful to waken

And too play some long ball, to get seats to swing
And with the next census, change redistricting

TRUMP'S MODEL PLAIN

First mocks, then embraces, his signature moves
His M.O., disruption, for him this behooves

He trusts few will like him, and we can see why
Just supporters believing, "pie in the sky"

It's pure vintage Trump, not that hard to see
With him all is *BAD*, with no capital "T"

He'll talk things down sharply, so when he steps in
He'll then sing it's praises, now in his mind, a win

Of party, convention, and the election
Squawks of rigging, conspiracy, and deception

It's really quite simple, strategy succinct
"Preemptive accusations", makes others shrink

Then on the defensive, and backpedaling
He stole your offense, while you're defending

So wise up America, to his lies and distractions
And call him on nonsense, and manipulative actions

THE MAN DOTH PROTEST TOO MUCH*

So early on, Trump paved the way
For love of comrade, come what may

It's been his constant, proclamation
With each new tweet, a condemnation

Defending Russia, and his pal Vlad
Against *Intelligence*, very SAD

What really is, his motivation
To bind to this, bad actor's nation

He pushes hard, at every turn
To soft sell Putin, while allies, burn

"Da", we know, there is a connection
Political *kapital*, spent for protection

Whatever it is, will find its way out
Confirm his character, without any doubt

With poetic justice, here's your failure's link
You've protested too much, we all clearly think

*Inpired by the line from Shakespeare's Hamlet
"The lady doth protest too much, methink."

TRUMP MODEL TOO

He bullshits and bullies, but never backs down
Though he'll *walk it back*, when advantage not found

His approach incorporates, a Catch-22
If he's wins, it's all him, if not, it's on you

He understands legal, so well from his side
The laws that constrain him, are those you'll abide

The ones that impede him, he'll push, bend, or break
His payoffs determine, the risks that he'll take

His cadre of lawyers, do their job so well
For most human beings, a real living hell

And when he goes bankrupt, it ain't no big thing
He'll write off losses, still no tax he'll bring

His obsession is endless, he can't help but come back
And if you don't succumb, he's on the attack

Urine for it Now

"The President of, all Americans"
Is a fact, not a pledge, as Trump begins

Full representation, he so implies
As few get favored, masses get lies

With inauguration, two days away
We've now a cabinet, that's *pay to play*

Tax breaks for wealthy, no funding for schools
Gut E.P.A. safeguards, they take us for fools

Strange love for Putin, yet China gets none
Rumors of misdeeds, urination for fun

Conflicts of interest, with family and business
So Kafkaesque, can I get a witness

Slams civil rights lead, on M.L.K. day
Suspect stock trades, that don't seem OK

No fearing of hearings, from these nominees
They don't answer questions, just say what they please

Equivocating, then sly smiles unfurl
The spin reminiscent; a Tilt-a-Whirl

Did you vote for change, know it's almost here
Not, the good kind, but the other, I fear

In The Bag; Sad

Inauguration, it's in the bag
Like most Trump speeches, it made us gag

So many tropes, that won't come true
"Never let you down", that time is through

Words do matter, yet he still cares not
Absent integrity, trust will rot

He's still selling goods, to those in pain
With rhetoric alone, just applause he'll gain

Insists on calling, America broken
As things aren't great, till on them he's spoken

And what's with all the, "Here and Now"
To start and stop things, Holy Cow!

Enough with all these, proclamations
And absolutes, with no reservations

He's now the President, to many a faction
Post-purchase-dissonance*, most folk's reaction

*Post purchase dissonance;
after a purchase, the buyer undergoes post purchase dissonance, meaning the
buyer regrets his /her purchase.

FIRST COLD PRESSER

First press conference, served *Spicer whine*
Mistreatment of his guy, all the time

Claims the press, is too negative
As Trump's tells lies, on which world does he live

Cherry picks one tweet, with a mistruth
Of lies and falsehoods, Trump's the Babe Ruth

He demeans, insults, and proselytizes
At best, on occasion, "Apple-a-gizes"

So Sean is working, from Trump's playbook
Claims unfair treatment, setting the hook

And fair-minded folks, find themselves bending back
Once relinquish ground, open to attack

The Dems fell for this, let's hope Press is smarter
Avoiding this pitfall, and *press* on much harder

And just for the record, Sean changed his words
In regards to crowds, it's all now absurd

"Both in person and, around the world"
Conveys two records, means this pearl

Then resells it, "All eyeballs combined"
He must hope we're stupid, or small of mind

Kudos to Rather, warns the, Fourth Estate
Honor the office, scorn whom, intimidate

Unnerving, and not yet Deserving

Of the adage, "a man's word is his bond"
For people of honor, of that saying they're fond

Don't shift paradigms, or change how we score
Don't lie to us, falsehoods we abhor

It's strange when asked, to know what you mean
To look in your heart, like a girl of thirteen

Though it makes much sense, when we see how you *tweet*
At your stage of life, it's not cute or sweet

Intentions are one thing, yet truth is another
Show you know the difference, still with lies you smother

Enough of hyperbole, you won the sale
Now will you deliver, or be an, epic fail

You ran for attention, knowing you couldn't win
But external forces, threw the monkey wrench in

Now to all's dismay, we find ourselves here
Wouldn't it be great, to instill hope, not fear

FOUND AND LOST

Dear Mr. President, you're being an ass
You use words like elegant, then ones most crass

Still things you're debating, matter not at all
And with your peevishness, you make yourself small

Only you know you're perfect, all of us know you lie
So just focus on work, *Presidential*, please try

Perhaps you could once, bully all others' thinking
Now your statements outlandish, and can't blame them on
drinking

Crowd size, voter fraud, and electoral win rankings
The facts are against you, so you must like these spankings

So appear as a child, who can't get his way
Shining light on delusions, that won't go away

Then shame will sink in, almost being *The Man*
Lost it all over ego, congrats on that plan

"Duh Donald"

You're true to your ways, because they got you here
Though legitimacy, remains your biggest fear

You take so much credit, though privately doubt
Knowing forces at work, will soon be called out

Causality is how, experts have described
If something's impacted, by a factor allied

But your ego dictates, you were the sole cause
In winning the election, though you should take pause

Count politics as usual, Clinton born hate
Or D.N.C. mischief, Bernie fans left irate

Or those disillusioned, saying, "go drain the swamp"
Their throwaway votes, got a Cabinet of pomp

Take F.B.I. timing, or select Russian hacking
Or voters nonplussed, of candidates so lacking

I suppose your denial, leaks in truth's light
As persistent facts, confirm you're not right

Talk electoral rankings, vote margins, crowd size
You should know the nation, sees right through your lies

So stop talking mandate, majority support
Your party couldn't stand you, "Never Trump" did purport

The Speaker and leaders, have fallen in place
As sycophants come crawling, to earn a space

Don't think they revere you, as they lay at your feet
As they'll use you to suckle, on the government teat

CAN YOU EAR THIS

To the big cheese at Disney, let us be clear
And take this to heart, with a big mouse ear

Your social contract, we all embrace
You're about inclusion, of the whole human race

For generations, our trust you've earned
Our kids placed in your hands, and never burned

But at this time, the norms have changed
Values and reality, now rearranged

Where hateful speech, and degradation
Are common place, from the head of our nation

So we ask that you, now take a stand
And join our families, across this land

And in The Great Hall, of Presidents
Mute speech of the latest, of residents

If not, show him for, what he is
And let his words show, where his heart lives

Protect the ideals, of our American Way
Have the newest animatronic, have nothing to say

DeTrimental DeVos

Now let's debate, Betsy DeVos
Who's nomination, will be our loss
As it seems, she knows not, what she stands for

Not degree'd, in education
With no teaching, certification
Yet it's clear, public schools, she does abhor

Highly touts, the charter school
And in her world, vouchers rule
Yet she flip-flopped, repeatedly, on Common Core

Kudos Collins, and Murkowski
From G.O.P. rule, they've broken free
Earning our praise, worthy of, a Senator

Perhaps you voted, party lines
Afraid McConnell, will steal your dimes
If so, you're just a, money grubbing whore

Maybe DeVos, bought your nod
A contribution, from her fat wad
As billionaires, hurt us, to our very core

So to others, grow a pair
Do the right thing, show you care
Or know, you won't likely, serve one term more

As most people, in this country
From Public Ed, they just can't flee
Yet from voting booths, they'll settle, every score

BALLISTIC DUH-PLOMACY

It's been said North Koreans, are really quite small
But with I.C.B.M.s, they quickly grow tall

Their missiles are flying, going further each time
From the Winter Whitehouse, Trump assures things are fine

I guess we should trust him, as he is so well rested
With two trips to Florida, in three weeks, since vested

And on, Kim Jong-un, how bad is this man
Sure he lies, and sounds crazy, has his own travel ban

He's good friends with Russia, and a NATO detractor
Delusional, narcissistic, with no Free Press to factor

With speech that inflames, and rhetoric so threatening
It all sounds familiar, and will bring it's own reckoning

I'm surprised that our President, hasn't called him with glee
They've so much in common, could it be pure envy

This requires a statesman, perhaps Trump, freshly tan
If not him, get an expert, and call Dennis Rodman

MISTRESS KELLY OF THE DARK LORD

What is the half-life, of Kellyanne Conway
Who drops lies like litter, on our TVs' byway

How many times, can she really call foul
Then spin and pivot, clutching her crying towel

Our gag reflex to her, has become so acute
As most of her comments, we quickly refute

Her goodwill has run out, with repute now ill
As formidable forces, show her word's worth nil

She acts with temerity, signed her pact with Satan
Made bold by momentum, which is quickly abatin'

Though she can't jump ship, of her own volition
To her Dark Lord that's treason, under every condition

If lucky, she'll get fired, else down with the ship
That won't pay her debt, for attaching, to his hip

#TRUMPCAKE

This Trump cake, looks like a mistake
A hot mess, of red, white, and blue

It's gaudy, looks fake, like it's very namesake
To preserve it, he'll probably sue

Now what can be done, with nine layers of fun
Will alternative ideas, you eschew

Perhaps first assault it, when it caves, exalt it
Then a cabinet post, we'll all rue

Put it up for sale, as upscale retail
Exclusively, at Nordstrom, for a few

Hunt it down on the veldt, for its rich fondant pelt
Let the Trump boys shoot, and kill this too

But for heaven's sake, please don't serve this cake
Indigestion, will likely, ensue

GENERAL VALENTINE DAY MASSACRE

With General Flynn, let the carnage begin
And soon, there'll be several more
Once the details are in, on his Russian based sin
Finger pointing, will cut to the core

With so much confusion, and leaks that are oozin'
This administration's start, is piss poor
Trump bluffed and threatened, and is now surely frettin'
As he learns now, what he has in store

Although in charge fully, the courts he can't bully
Still he sabotages, his own rapport
Count "One China" folly, Japan handshakes too jolly
Voter fraud, from his fantasies galore

His spokespeople lampooned, while he plays buffoon
While the G.O.P., watches in horror
Goldman Sachs now takes over, turning swamp into clover
It's the coup, that he warned of before

Then with all of those factions, comes sad interactions
So bad blood, leaves them settling the score
But it's not over yet, there's still too much to fret
They'll impeach him, then show him the door

LABOR'S DISFAVOR

Puzder's dead, or nomination instead
Is it paperwork lacking, or what he has said

Know he's not a fan, of a minimum wage
Prefers robots to people, not labor sage

Domestic violence, keeps popping up
Abuse your wife once, and it's more than enough

Andy's workers at home, are undocumented
Those labor regulations, are not lamented

This gig wasn't for you, you should be quite grateful
Go hang out with models, far from speech so hateful

So please carry-on, peddle burgers with sex
We'll fear your replacement, Trump's worst choice, comes next

LET'S STIPULATE YOU'RE NOT

Perhaps now is the time, to make some things clear
You're not the least or most, of what you claim dear

You're certainly not, the most presidential
You've most room for improvement, if not potential

You're "a really smart person", comes with doubt
Though anxiously we wait, to have that proved out

And "smarter than the generals", we'll put that to rest
Secret plans to beat ISIS, that was more Trump BS

So what of the "less than's", of Race and Semitic
Those statements insulting, and truly pathetic

You handle bad stories, better than all
You should be quite practiced, as you tell tales so tall

Your Electoral record, was now something you "heard"
It's not even close, again truth you've blurred

On the cover of "Time", not a record, too
Nor your first 30 days, with accomplishments few

And when the dust settles, "The Most" record you had
Is the number of supporters, that were lied to. SAD

READING LABELS

Trump shares at a rally, you label opponents
A practiced strategy, with grade school proponents

Cruel playground taunting, shouldn't be the norm
Of this Trump's a master, sporting Olympic form

He disrespects people, party, and the race
For that he's the President, so enough, "in-your-face"

Once grown, childish things, we should leave behind
We communicate better, show respect and act kind

Without civil discourse, we'd get nothing done
We've comedians, to inject life with fun

So come on Mr. President, I'm so irked to say
Since you're not eight years old, consider what you say

MOURNING WOOD

It's clear now why, Trump is so perturbed
It's his Propecia, growing hair so absurd

He's so in love, with his faux comb-over
So reminiscent, of my Afghan Hound, Rover

Though side effects, may be wreaking havoc
As sexually, it's a below-the-waist, car wreck

Impotence, and, sexual indifference
Orgasms lost, makes this P-grabber, real tense

The good news is, that hands often do swell
Else he'd sign with two hands, not quite presidential

So pretty please Donald, let go of your hair
Being bald, sane, and virile, is an exchange that's fair

DEFERENTIAL AND REFERENTIAL

Trump says it himself, he just likes to win
No matter the contest, or prevailing wind

Yet his bandwidth is narrow, on things presidential
His talking points scattered, with most referential

He does not know government, intimately
And from most issues, he'd like to flee

The depth and the breath, of bureaucracy immense
So he'll focus on immigrants, and wall, soon a fence

So he's got the big chair now, but won't do the work
He'll watch lots of TV, and reading he'll shirk

He'll defer to Bannon, Pence, and Ryan
And to his cabinet, a likely buy-in

So do people use him, the answer, bigly
He's there for the reverence, conflict, and intrigue

He loves things distressed, best domain for a bully
So he talks things down, takes advantage of, fully

This old dog's energetic, but mentally he's through
He finally bit off, more than he can chew

Revolting Voters, Rebuked Representatives

Spicey claims they're loud, and for that he's dismissive
Or calls them *professionals*, since they're not submissive

Says some folks are angry, seems he's got a clue
Holding feet to fire, is what we need to do

Poor Congressman Chaffetz, claims intimidation
Interrupting land deals, as he sells off our nation

And to Spicey claims, that protesters are paid for
Like voter fraud claims, more Trumpian behavior

If you watch town halls, you can feel people's pain
Legislators don't like it, here careers can get slain

The smart ones attend, but don't dare leave early
And respect every voter, if polite, or if surly

This country's awakening, re-finding it's voice
We've suffered this Congress, having had little choice

An organized revolt, a la, Arab Spring
Using social media, and the power it'll bring

GOP Hedging on Pledging

I pledge allegiance, to the flag
To have this pledge, be so damn glad

Of the United States, of America
With a divided government, in hysteria

And to the republic, for which it stands
Of The Rule of Law, our founders were fans

One nation, under God, indivisible
Don't respect this, our lives become miserable

With liberty, and justice for all
Shame, G.O.P. dropped this, our rallying call

INDEPENDENT OR END IT

We need a counsel, who is quite independent
For investigations, not McConnell dependent

If you've worried about leverage, the Russians might hold
Fear Mitch owning Don, a coup, not yet told

One way or another, Trump's going down
He's erratic, un-American, and mentally unsound

The Congress will end him, or could be the Courts
Maybe those feigning loyal, a betrayal of sorts

Perhaps Trump will step down, to avoid new elections
So Pence can take over, heading off insurrections

Will the Dems quickly cave, do "what's best for the nation"
Based on G.O.P.'s urging, without hesitation

Priebus, gets a talk show, with Spicey co-host
Kellyanne goes postal, Bannon now a ghost

With C.I.A., F.B.I., N.S.A., and more
We'll know what we're made of, what government stands for

PRESUMPTIVE AND PETULANT

Presumptive and petulant, a bad combination
They're Trump's strongest traits, and they threaten the nation

He creates false realities, polarizes his core
With his alternate facts, I call "Trumpian Lore"

He'll pre-accused many, of many a thing
It's a devious strategy, in hopes he'll be King

Nomination is rigged, and too, the election,
The G.O.P. plots, for the press, no protection

And those racist, or sexist, or anti-Semitic
He won't denounce them, as things turn frenetic

As Bannon reminds him, this is his loyal base
And if he calls them out, his support, he'll erase

NOBODY KNEW

"Nobody Knew", and by that, you meant you
It's clear you're clueless, to what's wrong

When you talk of insurance, you reveal incoherence
With your random thoughts, you string along

How your uninformed view, sticks in your brain like glue
To learn more, your commitment need be strong

As you never have dealt, with the pain most have felt
High premiums/co-pays, all yearlong

Know that each time you speak, we pull our hair and shriek
From your brain farts, where real facts, belong

"Great healthcare, at a tiny fraction of the cost"
"It's going to be so easy"
- Donald J. Trump, 2016

ONE GUY'S REBUTTAL –
1ST JOINT ADDRESS 2017

Clearly, G.O.P., put out the call
Stand and clap, or from favor you'll fall

They want to give Trump, one bragging right
With an applause record, no one can fight

The camera pans, but smiles you don't see
On Republican leaders, few clapping freely

The Supreme Court Justices, look like they're sick
As people of honor, they don't like things slick

For every new "Reg", two must now go
I guess three's too many, and one-half, too low

"America's torch, will light up the world"
Or burn our bridges, as his plans are unfurled

He talks immigration, McConnell stone-faced
Perhaps he'd be happy, with just the white race

A reference to Ike's, infra-structure bill
One Supreme Commander, One bone spurs made ill

So there's, *Hire American*, and buy the same
It sounds good to hear, implementing is lame

He'll lower the cost, of your health insurance
But words ring false, as he gives no assurance

Access guaranteed, pre-existing condition
Not saying affordable, important, by omission

Health care costs reduced, code for tort reform
So doctors aren't liable, when they don't perform

So he'll build infrastructure, and military
With tax breaks for all, how can this be

So let's slash restraints, at all agencies
"Then kids grow with miracles", is that plain to see?

Funding, school choice, for Hispanic and Black
Will tax credits help, if income you lack

The murder rate highest, in about fifty years
A truthful statistic, or one that he hears

Proudly proclaims, record Defense spending
And as an aside, Veterans' needs, never-ending

Then proclaims that he represents, every state
With his lies and deceit, we cannot relate

He speaks the right words, contradicting his actions
It all rings so hollow, knowing him and his factions

Under the Guise, in Front of the Eyes, of the People

At Newport News shipyards, Marine One lands
On a Ford Class Carrier, wait five-thousand hands

Going off script again, asks for agreement
To stay on script, his greatest achievement

A ton of superlatives, hands them out like candy
He'd hug every woman, this President so randy

Hand wave, fist pump, thumb pump, point
Small hands so active, leveraging each joint

Steps from the lectern, claps and mouths, "Thank You"
Sailor paparazzi, with their cell phones, not few

It's reality TV, and it all seems absurd
With a captive audience, he loves to be heard

Funny-Bone Unknown

Trump's never seen laughing, but he'll smirk and gloat
Sounds like Snidely Whiplash, when he casts his vote

He has no sense of humor, when the joke's on him
Perhaps he's too literal, can't enjoy "on a whim"

Doesn't says things with humor, at best quips ironic
But unless you're a loyalist, he just sounds moronic

As a narcissist, there's no, self-deprecating
Doesn't bond one-on-one, can't do, friendly relating

Self-obsessed, cold-blooded, and always promoting
So he talks in hyperbole, praising or goading

He's shy that one gene, where we enjoy laughter
Despised "the before", how you liking "the after"

FAT MAN AND LITTLE BOY

Bannon and Miller, legislative composers
In Canadian parlance, a couple of *Hosers*

Sure, McCartney and Lennon, had thee greatest hits
But if you like crazy, go with Trump's two dipshits

You can't talk great duos, without Hall and Oates
But the duo of Steves, is a terd flushed, that floats

Think dynamic duo, Batman and Boy Wonder
Well these two ain't them, tearing government asunder

So good riddance to both, the sooner the better
If Trump fires you, it's a short, well signed letter

LIARS ARE DENIERS

Liars are deniers, show no surprise
That's how they sustain, their basket of lies

They act with contempt, when they are confronted
They can't stand the scrutiny, when truth is hunted

When you blow their cover, they'll have to move on
They'll find a new audience, whom of them, is fond

They'll again commence weaving, their web of deceit
Working their agenda, this is how they compete

And if too successful, they'll reach the top
And once outed there, their lies finally stop

THE DON OF DELUSION

"Don't know if, he'll admit it, he [Barack] likes me"
We're sure he never did, as most clearly see
When you treat someone poorly, they're not prone to adore thee
So swallowing their contempt, is most likely

Mistaking, no resistance, for compliance
To serve agendas, most won't show defiance
As a crucial time will come, they'll all beat the same drum
As your frenemies will now share, a strong alliance

Of course you're not welcome, in that group
Past transgressions, keep you out of the loop
Now weakened and exposed, with knives sharp, and fists closed
As with Caesar, your Senators, will swoop

GREAT AGAIN?

What is the "Great", in "Great Again"
Why should we have to guess
Was it the age of Robber Barons
Where for *most*, they had less

And lend a clue, on *Law and Order*
We're not sure, we must confess
Demographics change perception
No answer, even when, you press

Let's face it, these are slogans
Not policies, so refined
These themes are universal
And so, not well defined

So people now have voted
For their versions, of these phrases
This feels like a catastrophe
In these earliest, of stages

So own your vote, accept your part
Your scrutiny, was it wise
But as of now, it seems quite clear
Trump's promises, were lies

Obamacare, now not so bad
Perhaps it needs, a tweak
"Lock her up," he's over that
Or of this, still he'll speak

How 'bout that wall, made of concrete
That Mexico will to pay for
It's just his norm, to say what works
Speaks lies as truth, there'll be more

Ryan's Triad: Prongs, Phases, and Parts

I'm watching Paul Ryan, with his PowerPoint show
He's emphatic and urgent, to make this vote go

With his three prong approach, to replace and repeal
It's like watching a huckster, so nauseous you'll feel

He's prepared and deliberate, as he makes each point
But it's process, not product, of this plan he'll anoint

Oops, now they're *phases*, or is it three *parts*
It's like trying to read tea leaves, with mystical arts

It's not insurance, but tax breaks for the rich
As Ryan, their water boy, hopes we'll be their bitch

WEALTHY TAX BREAK? MISTAKE!

Do the ultra wealthy, really get a tax break
Come on, stop kidding, this must be a mistake

Do the top 10%, need a cash infusion
Tell those with nothing, and watch their confusion

With the national debt, at now record highs
We don't have it to give, what a surprise

Instead of huge tax breaks, give people healthcare
You'll stimulate spending, and save folks, from despair

Weren't you for the people, the regular guy
Giving tax breaks to wealthy, deserves our outcry

So it's pipelines, walls, and military spending
Corporate taxes, and Regs, get the *happy ending*

You've duped your supporters, kiss rallies goodbye
Das Vedanya comrade Trump, to the Kremlin, say, "Hi"

Donny Darko Soon to Go

Quit worrying about, Trump's Republican cover
They're backing away, soon on Pence they will hover

I've said it before, and I'll say it again
They'll keep him around, till his useful end

They excel not at leading, but falling in line
With eight years of obstruction, they're now on the dime

Being sidelined this long, they should have better plans
To tear down is easy, now build something, that stands

They are well positioned, to run things for years
But the midterms will crush them, and confirm all their fears

Don't make their mistake, instead now be constructive
And in so, renew faith, and be civically instructive

No Drama vs. All Trauma

No drama Obama, where did you go
You left us with Trump, a veritable shit show

You read, took your briefings, and were ever so clear
Trump peeks at one pagers, then his words instill fear

Your speeches were moving, your delivery was tight
Trump's bombastic, incoherent, and that's on a good night

Your family, a treasure, and Michelle makes us proud
Trump's clan gives pause, no matter, what they've vowed

You are decent and honorable, even self-deprecating
Trump is crass and vulgar, humorless and baiting

You spoke to the world, and put them at ease
Trump opens his mouth, and relations seize

You saved the economy, in the throes of distress
For which Trump takes credit, "inherited a mess"

So of course you are missed, even more than we thought
We prefer honest leaders, versus those Russian bought

A Figurative Approach to Literal vs. Serious

So they tell me that *literal*, has a new antonym
It used to be *figurative*, so from there let's begin

When you employ figurative, a representation
It implies similarity, a type of relation

It expresses a feeling, but not so much fact
You'd refrain from its use, where you need be exact

In matters of gravity, you'll need go literal
It's precise, and discreet, toward achieving your goal

It, avoids confusion, not ambiguous
One interpretation, with nothing amiss

It's the language of those, that need to be clear
When words matter most, and confusion brings fear

But now we have Trump, a circle not squared
Of his outbursts on Twitter, we all should be spared

But as, President, his words carry weight
And with his impulse issues, so goes our fate

So by clever phrase, we have "literal or serious"
They are not opposing, to suggest so, insidious

We simply can't change, word definitions
To appease Donald Trump's, vague predilections

Nor should we, normalize, to his strange ways
Then we too will ramble, around in his haze

Let's agree he should be, literal and serious
We don't need a leader, irrational and delirious

"You have to take things like that seriously and literally."
-Senator Lindsey Graham
031517 18:07
MSNBC interview by Greta Van Susteren

REPUBLICS 101

Congratulations to the French, if only now, two thirds
It seems you listen to candidates, and still, you value words

You assess their backgrounds, and gauge character
Accepting no false pledges, or hate, that they stir

You learned from the lesson, of our recent election
And heeded the damage, of Russian connection

Though facing tough issues, you stood strong, and chose order
Our electorate reactive, dumped baby, and bath water

You've preserved liberty, something we now fight for
And on equality, we'll work more than before

You're a great nation, our country's first friend
And we'll be "Great Again", when Trump comes to an end

HEARINGS START FEARINGS*

Shame on the hacks, from the G.O.P.
Who conduct themselves, so frivolously

They're laying down cover, semantically
With fallacies even, a child could see

Oh, Chairman Nunes, how do you sleep
Will Ryan, fire you, if his faith you don't keep

You're now committing, the cardinal sin
Party before country, with nothing to win

Know that your voters, are seeking the facts
Each statement uttered, strong logic it lacks

Your questions loaded, witnesses opine
How long have you beaten, this deceased equine

Manipulative queries, fuel Trump's lying tweets
Have you found your soul mate, in this man that cheats

Perhaps you and Spicer, can now share a shrink
And if no peace there, you can both take up drink

But when this goes bad, you'll wish you stood tall
As President Schiff, now won't take your call

* I know it's not a word!

No Votes to Spare on TrumpCare

To congressional members, planning to vote
On Ryan's health bill, please now, take note

We know you've been pressured, by Paul, Don, and Mitch
Though we didn't elect you, to become their bitch

You know this bill's wrong, and what it'll do
So stand to the pressure, that's why we chose you

Else, blood's on your hands, and you'll regret it fully
Tens of millions will suffer, if you cave to each bully

It wasn't the billionaires, who gave you your seat
So why do you serve them, and party elite

Do the words, "People's House", even ring true
As 700,000, put their faith in you

Understand, "Representative", is what we need see
We the people, of your district, not the powers that be

Know your leadership's leaders, have put their foot down
And you are expendable, for their new money found

We're not that naïve, at least not on this bill
And if you don't serve us, your job, soon we'll fill

We don't buy rationale, that this works in prong three
Because that's textbook crap, even we now can see

So there's nowhere to hide, betwixt rock and hard place
You can honor your Office, or live on in disgrace

THEATER OF THE ABSURD

Neil Gorsuch, oh shucks, wow, gee whiz
It's Mayberry talk, is that where he lives

He's more cornpone, then we've seen in a while
Gosh darn, holy cow, then a, big dang smile

Loves to, reminisce, about Justices past
Anecdotes of greatness, 'bout names that won't last

He repeats and revisits, just what a judge is
With emphatic one liners, defining his biz

Eschews things political, claims it's not germane
Yet to Rightwing causes, he's affixed his name

So stop with nostalgia, spare us *mutton busting*
Answer questions forthrightly, or find us, not trusting

PODIUM PROSTITUTION

Sean Spicer now qualifies, as a prostitute
Pleasures just one *john* Donald, a crazy coot

His first time out, was no grand slam home run
Wore a suit coat too big, sweating too much for fun

Trump took him to task, in a much public way
As Sean's odds 50-50, whether he'd go or stay

With his new job in peril, he sucked it up
Then treatment, of reporters, turned quite abrupt

He'll equivocate, lie, and prevaricate
Misdirect and confuse, at all these, he's first rate

Yet some Press still like him, aware of his *pickle*
Know he chose to serve Trump, his master so fickle

Does he rationalize, that someone must do it
Is it worth all the shame, to be Trump's conduit

His reward likely infamy, and perhaps a book deal
What's the cost of one's honor, where truth once had appeal

If you lay down with dogs, likely you'll rise with fleas
Lie too long for this President, you'll contract his disease

Oh Me, Oh My, but Why?

The Senate Republicans, stand up and whine
Oh no, not a filibuster, they now opine

These privileged white man, each take a few moments
To perpetuate their myth, of unjust opponents

It's never been done, to Scotus nominee
Denied Garland outright, filibustered virtually

Chairman Grassley begins, seeming confounded
Shame on you Charles, to truth you're not bonded

More Oren Hatch moaning, "Oh Gosh," he'll exclaim
Points to the "Far Left", and on them he lays blame

"D's get their judges, R's never get theirs"
Cries Lindsey Graham, sparing requisite tears

In the background they chuckle, as each takes his turn
Is this *conduct unbecoming*, of this, what should we learn

They're claiming high ground, a deceitful act
Towards their "nuclear option", plan of attack

"A dangerous precedent", all parties agree
McConnell brought us here, so accountable, he'll be

BOOB-TUBE LUBED

Our TV-tied president, viewed horrific acts
Where men-women-children, suffer Sarin attacks

It's not the first gassing, or the second, or third
As Trump feigns empathy, he looks so absurd

He's known this for years, and warned to stay away
So let's question motives, more distraction I say

He'll focus on "babies", to sell his outrage
His language so *loaded*, to take center stage

He jumps into action, starts blaming Obama
Resolute in his lying, shameless leverage, for drama

On his Nth trip to Florida, hosting President Xi
Unilaterally bombs Syria, so illegally

It's a hard 180, from his tweets of the past
Like most of his utterances, meanings don't last

Some people praise him, I remain skeptical
It has Vlad's fingerprints, dia-bol-i-cal

A cool hundred million, is the latest tally
The taxpayer's ante, for applause, next rally

But consider the damage, we're now told, not bad
That airfield, operational, failed Op, so SAD

And the *heads-up* to Russians, just an hour before
Warns all co-conspirators, hardly settling a score

Does this pass your "smell test", or the stench you don't mind
Putin plays chess, Trump checkers, and staying blind

FAILED STATE OF MINDLESSNESS

The "Holocaust Centers", is what Spicer said
A sanitized name, where millions, killed dead

Seems his Hitler comparison, was just not enough
German Jews were gassed, is history that tough

He's told many lies, often obfuscating
Gets tongue tied and clumsy, disorientating

He'll butcher a word, when syllables count three
Proper nouns, live in fear, acronyms try to flee

When he references history, often it's a bad choice
Yet somehow he's perfect, to channel Trump's voice

Asking for forgiveness, he adds fuel to the fire
For his mental health, perhaps he should retire

Tax Day's Foul Filing

No Taxes from Trump, gets a big loud *harrumph*
One more campaign pledge, we'll never see

One-hundred towns strong, people, march along
Against lies, and no transparency

Perhaps they'll show loans, which in turn create moans
Confirming, suspicions, clearly

Of each Russian connection, before the election
His advisers lost, now total three

So give this lying chicken, one more wound, worth licking
Keep protesting, till we reach, victory

Dear Mr. President

President Trump, the greatest, of all time
Of course, you think so, it's all in your mind

You've done almost nothing, but make a big fuss
Your *Executive Orders*, fool none of us

You've a G.O.P. Congress, that won't go your way
No serious legislation, up till today

So fall back on Gorsuch, you picked from a list
McConnell went nuclear, or on that, you'd have missed

Your numbers are falling, your lies have worn thin
Your prospects quite SAD, the verdict is in

We know you can't change, and you're so ill equipped
Your impotence welcome, on most issues, you've flipped

So please, while you're here, don't break anything
As your First 100 Days, preview messes you'll bring

SURVIVING TRUMP'S WORDS

To Holocaust survivors, Trump gave his best speech
Spoke of truth and honor, both out of his reach

To recite words from paper, may help make things clear
But the way he flip-flops, for now, it quells fear

The Holocaust Remembrance, just a few months back
The word "Jews" went unmentioned, a slight, or attack

His White House has members, Neo Nazi, Alt-right
Backs French Le Pen, anti-Semite, in plain sight

Each action speaks volumes, louder than each word
Guilt by association, doesn't seem now, absurd

So before you embrace him, for this overdue speech
Make sure you consider, his commitment, it'll teach

TAX CUT AND RUN AMOK

Take a step back, and you will see
The motivations, of Trump policy

It's about protection, of the monied class
And the rest of America, can kiss his ass

He'll build the military, against insurrection
Is "never too big", the right direction

And reduces the government, to family and friends
Steals the *People's* voice, while transparency ends

As most of us struggle, knowing whom he'll serve
Those with great assets, with greed matching nerve

They'll gut healthcare, and pension plans
And social programs, of which they're not fans

The less we spend, the less they'll pay
Knowing our way of life, will soon slip away

Most people in power, are not your friends
They now own the country, here freedom ends

If things get too bad, they'll just move offshore
And our grand experiment, will be no more

They don't want to pay, for the benefits of you
Only legislation, for them, will get through

They're against the Death Tax, doesn't favor the wealthy
Singing middle-class tunes, then pass bills, quite stealthy

Cohn and Mnuchin, of thee Goldman Sachs
Trump rallied against, in his "swamp drain" attacks

These guys are quite brilliant, but no less self-serving
They're not there for us, in their eyes, not deserving

So they'll throw us some crumbs, but they'll hoard all the cake
If you think something different, that'll be your mistake

Sit by and do nothing, you'll get your, just reward
A chance for the scraps, as just one of the horde

Or join the resistance, debate, march, or tweet
Let's change Trump's direction, or else face defeat

THE NEXT HUNDRED DAYS

"Promises Made", "Promises Kept"
Slogans like these, show Trump's so inept

He went to PA, for his "Hundred Days" rally
To recall non-events, and give a false tally

To those not, of his base, but of the G.O.P.
They've distanced themselves, from this kleptocracy

His faithful trust him, won't see that he lies
They're committed, all in, there is no compromise

They bought what he sold, and abandoned all doubt
Now they hope against hope, that things will work out

Most are not deplorables, and most are not stupid
They put trust in a Con Man, as if matched by Cupid

They'll stay to the end, nowhere else now, to go
And rationalize their choice, although down deep, they know

Representative of Nothing

Did you vote for TrumpCare, of it what did you know
Did you read the whole bill, or just go with the flow

With no CBO scoring, you still joined along
Because Ryan and Trump, made you feel you belong

So you bowed to the pressure, and sold out your district
Afraid of your party, and the funds they would restrict

You've no clue of the costs, or folks impacted
You've done what you're told, to get this enacted

To satisfy angst, of your G.O.P. leaders
After two terms obstructing, healthcare now teeters

So premiums and deductibles, you claim you'll reduced
And save one trillion dollars, how's this logic deduced

And the savings, they'll mostly, go to the rich
While screwing Joe Public, with this deadly pitch

So congrats to lawmakers, that have voted *Yea*
With the midterms approaching, you've signed your seats away

Status Quo, Hell No

There's a word being used, with more frequency
It sounds quite innocuous, let's look and see

Some say it's boring, a synonym of average
It's flavor vanilla, you'd not think to disparage

So enough with the teasers, now this word I will share
It is "Normalizing", and it should invoke terror

The context is Trump, and his aberrant behavior
He's opaque, erratic, and he lies to gain favor

He tears down, destroys, and vilifies all
He's less of a president, and more wrecking ball

He's poisoned relations, with many world leaders
And established himself, as most asinine of tweeters

On all his behaviors, he sets the bar low
We can't normalize this, so he's gotta go

FRYING PAN INTO HELLFIRE

What kind of Christian, is Vice President Pence
Often lies by deception, where's his recompense

He'll praise and laud Trump, as if he were king
Will he sell out our country, for the treasures it'll bring

Don't conflate integrity, with soft-spoken
As we've come around, why has he not awoken

And I'm guessing stupidity, is not his affliction
Perhaps he bides time, during Trump's dereliction

He is next in line, and we worry about that
And the damage he'll do, under a MAGA hat

Of Trump's early choices, they haven't fared well
They've dropped like flies, as if you couldn't tell

Fear Pence will get fired, and replaced by McConnell
Then Trump gets impeached, that's how I, define hell

SEE YOURSELF OUT, OF OFFICE

Mr. President, may I please introduce
A man you know of, with a mouth fast and loose

He'll jump to conclusions, is quick with a slur
Changes his mind so often, his thoughts surely blur

His motives are suspect, no promises kept
Know serious people, find him most inept

His actions consequential, but not in a good way
It's hard to imagine, that he'll be here to stay

Not trusted by colleagues, and less so by staff
Each ending as a, sacri-ficial calf

Says, "Showboat", "Grandstander", to demean another
But these words define him, this is how, he takes cover

Simply, he's never wrong, nor apologizes
He attacks and conquers, then proselytizes

Many have joined him, bought into the dream
He's not a winner, as at first, it would seem

You understand now, why this guy has to go
Write a letter, resign, and end this shit show

HAPPY DAYS ARE NEAR AGAIN

We've reached that juncture, where impeachment is broached
Trump's run out of cover, Constitution encroached

Of all his heinous, self-inflicted wounds
It seems now at this point, he tweets no tunes

Perhaps Lawyered Up, as now well he should
His undoing coming, as we all knew it would

Obstruction of Justice, Oaths of Loyalty
Shared secrets with Russians, "with great surety"

A Counsel from Rosenstein, of the, Special breed
Prior FBI Chief, with credentials, we need

Trump's bullying manner, and love for contention
Has now met its match, with Mueller's retention

In Trump, Ryan says, "he has great confidence"
On most any subject, his words make us wince

G.O.P. naysayers, silent and glad
Now off the hot seat, their voters stay mad

This White House nightmare, will come to an end
When truth sees daylight, then the country can mend

MITCH FOR THE RICH

There's a specter of evil, in the Senate, it's clear
Like a cancer metastasized, your greatest fear

It should've been excised, 8 years ago
It grew so quickly, Obama moved slow

Conniving, underhanded, lacks morality
Bought and paid for by lobbies, not surprised, are we

It's name, Mitch McConnell, the majority leader
A world-class obstructionist, with minor in theater

Not big on the limelight, keeps his profile low
Speaks very little, Mississippi slow

But don't let that fool you, he pulls all the strings
And serves his rich donors, they get their brass rings

He's has an agenda, cares not for the nation
Power, his mistress, Democrats, his frustration

So now with both houses, and the Presidency
He won't do for America, just watch him and see

Act II, Great Healthcare for Few

Rally up citizens, and know what's at stake
A most unconscionable, healthcare mistake

As Republican leadership, cares not for you
And they prove it with healthcare, that favored so few

It's clear that they're serving, some well lobbied folk
As the bill that they've passed, was an insulting joke

They'll take our benefits, give breaks to the rich
And of our representatives, watch loyalties switch

We've the highest of premiums, and the lowest of care
Of developed countries, our system is rare

As all these nations, have coverage, universal
This makes things worse, an Obamacare, reversal

Don't make it a con game, with à la cart pricing
Pitching us, coverage options, selling it as plan icing

Choosing this path, down this road they'll take more
Be damned, not guessing, your next ailment in store

So let's go single-payer, join the world-at-large
Make healthcare a right, show the people are in charge

Don't Feed the Hand, That Bites You

Trump speaks to the trades, gets half-hearted applause
Perhaps screwing them over, is the likely cause

His *rep* among workers, is really abysmal
Their prospect for payment, has proved, to be dismal

It's not just a couple, a few, or a dozen
With thousands of lawsuits, you'll see there's no lovin'

As his fortune's based, on a Zero-Sum game
To achieve his success, he leaves others in pain

Just seek out his partners, if they're still around
Bound by non-disclosures, they can't make a sound

A few made a profit, most *holding the bag*
Get in bed with his deals, know the outcome, is BAD

TRUMP'S FLIP-FLOPPING, SHOWS NO SIGNS OF STOPPING

Just 'cause he says it, does not make it true
When tallied up, his truths are few

I'll break down the reasons, perhaps you'll agree
No doubt you've noticed, together let's see

Trump pandered to crazy, his earliest base
Religion, misogyny, nationalism, and race

He fed his deplorables, a diet of hate
These rallies were Klan like, his outrage the bait

He'll serve that which resonates, cares not for facts
As he has one metric, how his crowd reacts

Know he doesn't lead, but follows, from in front
He picks up their scent, as this old dog can hunt

A consummate salesman, a *confidence man*
Without conscience or scruples, quickly changing his plan

His premier tactic, disparage, what exists
This comes in two flavors, with both he persists

Flavor One, supplies leverage, to many a foe
They'll bend over backwards, to fairness show

Primaries, The Press, Convention, Obama
Preemptively, cries foul, with childlike drama

Flavor Two, boasts victory, of something not won
Declares things broken, then claims fixed, voila, done

NATO, IC, Economy, Healthcare
These *messes inherited*, now in good repair

If his flip is disturbing, and his flop brings you peace
Know he'll probably flip back, let your hopefulness cease

OBSERVE TRUMP'S LEARNING CURVE

"Who knew", you exclaimed, about O-bama-care
"It's not what you would think", of your China dare

It's hard to know what's up, are we at the brink
And there you are, working out, each golf swing kink

Seventeenth, round of golf, and tenth resort stay
What might you, "know or think", if you'd work not play

With a third, of your term spent, at your properties
You've not helped the country, just pocketed, fees

Government's barely staffed, your choices, so poor
You'd have made better picks, blindly going, door-to-door

Your "Secretary-of-Everything", and "Daughter-Wife" in tow
Won't contain the secret, that there's little you know

Your platitudes transparent, as well as, your faux slights
For lies told to our nation, they'll be reading you, your rights

No-Fault Sexual Assault

O'Reilly and Trump, they're on the same page
Where megalomania, spews out fake rage

At the heart of their being, is self-aggrandizing
Where sexual misconduct, gets tagged, womanizing

Rich white men with privilege, on their bully pulpits
Point fingers and bluster, where dissenters are culprits

O'Reilly's "No Spin Zone", Trump's lying, en masse
Their pandering shameless, fuels a national morass

Look at what they do, polarize and mislead
Dividing the country, serving their fame and greed

They'll be known as the benchmark, of what not to do
When all's said and done, good riddance, you two

END GAME, MORE OF THE SAME

For the sake of argument, let's now surmise
That investigators soon, close in on Trump's lies

Know, he'll maximize, and get what he can
As it's his nature, of this conniving man

So his boys travel broadly, to lock down each deal
Before he is busted, for his final reveal

Then there's Jarred-Ivanka, his duo dynamic
With sweet access to leaders, making scores, so titanic

Sure the dust will fly, and there'll be a mess
He'll be impeached, pardoned, yet the truth, he won't fess

He'll live on in infamy, yell to those, who'll listen
Still red-faced and bold, his most natural, condition

History's Repeatings,
Serves Us More Beatings

At the risk of repeating, an earlier theme
We must all acknowledge, Trump is on his own team

He's officially against, all Obama stood for
He's righting a slight, to even a score

Though he's using the country, this childish man
He's negotiated nothing, this king of flimflam

He lacks comprehension, of what the job takes
As he proves with each utterance, that precedes his mistakes

Never accountable, and never wrong
So his staff suffers for him, this expendable throng

So the line of job seekers, is less than impressive
An understaffed White House, grows ever more restive

He trusts very few, because he can't be trusted
Because of this flaw, relations have rusted

So he tries to destroy things, that don't share his name
If you trusted he'd change, you've yourself to blame

Can't Conceive, Better Believe

Our Founding Fathers, in no way could conceive
What we every day, ourselves don't believe

We've a president intent, on ruining the nation
Lacking honor and truth, and deliberation

He fights for himself, and against all others
Petulant, selfish, just to have his druthers

He's worked to make enemies, of our allies
Dictators, he'll befriend, in front of our eyes

He won't staff the government, or bring in pros
It's sycophants and *yes-men*, that he's chose

Whom "speaks truth to power", in this cabal
The answer unknown, likely no one at all

He's outmatched, outplayed, his worst enemy
An epic embarrassment, to "The Land of the Free"

MERITS BADGE OF SHAME

Donald Trump speaks, to the B.S.A.
Inappropriate, is what, he chose to say

His behavior, contrary, to the Scout Pledge
Talks mostly in lies, and with truth he'll hedge

Gave his rally speech, to this group of boys
He bragged and attacked, traits he most enjoys

A Jamboree's not, the place for his spin
Scout leaders endorsed him, just having him in

All standing invites, need to be rescinded
To this conceited man, who's crass and ill-winded

To this great institution, of which I've belonged
You've let it get sullied, and in so, be wronged

Your small print will claim, his views are his own
Kids don't understand that, for this, now atone

Trump doesn't practice, good citizenship
His merit badge graphic, B.S.A.'s bloodied lip

Omnipotent or Impotent

Trump has now sold us, a whole lot of shit
If you've paid attention, you see he's unfit

He's lied with great ease, to each campaign stage
Even G.O.P. rivals, he'd come to assuage

He lured them in, with unbridled bravado
With third-grade name-calling, and one campaign motto

And they couldn't wait, to declare their allegiance
Not thinking that victory, would lead to malfeasance

Their loyalty oaths, he's demanded, define
A one-way commitment, they're finding, with time

Those blindly obedient, have sealed their fate
If they've crossed the line, they must stay and wait

As only a pardon, will set those folks free
Though if not related, there's slim chance for thee

SCREWED THE MOOCH

I think that I shall never see
Chaos as, this White House, be

With bodies falling, left and right
It reminds one of, a saloon fight

The Mooch comes on, Spicey resigns
A "Clean Slate" gesture, that Trump designs

The Mooch got vulgar, with the press
Trump didn't care, he'd quietly fess

Sure, Preibus lost, his good friend Sean
And within a week, he too is gone

He got the news, in a Friday tweet
Thanked Trump later, extra sweet

Now General Kelly, is Chief of Staff
Oh Mooch get ready, here's the laugh

Even though hired, but not sworn in
Your White House career, may never begin

INSANE NAME, OF BUDGET FAME

"A New Foundation, for American Greatness"
The name of this travesty, by those so mendacious*

This budget plan's in, and Ryan is thrilled
Mulvaney quite proud, of farm towns killed

But wait that's not all, there's the old and sick
And the GOP leaders, they don't give a lick

But what about those, who're food insecure
They'll be hurt by cuts, of that we're sure

And hope you're not, one somehow disabled
Hoped for no cuts, then that that was tabled

Let's say all these cuts, don't affect you
Know this slashes programs, which then serve few

What of Medicaid, Medicare, S.S.I.
Trump's promise to spare them, was spit in your eye

With cuts so draconian, it's one more tax break
If you think it's for you, you've made a mistake

*Mendacious
: given to or characterized by deception or falsehood or divergence from
absolute truth

Hammer Time* for a Change

It's been opined, classics, never die
Now never truer, on this we'll rely

Let's recognize he, wearing parachute pants
With his powerful lyrics, and one-line rants

They're steeped in ego, and self promotion
And perfect for Trump, before his demotion

The first is the premise, on how Trump has acted
It's called "Can't Touch This"*, a delusion protracted

It's arrogance, gaul, and bravado unending
But with honor and promises, Trump's just pretending

The follow up line, "Too Legit, to Quit"*
Not wearing so well, and soon it won't fit

As S.C. Mueller, will bring truth to light
Then find Trump exposed, his crimes in plain sight

So M.C. we thank you, for phrases so fine
Repurposed today, standing the test of time

*Lyrics/Titles by M.C. Hammer

Your White is Not Right

Once again Trump, addresses the nation
With his singular purpose, a standing ovation

Law-enforcement and military, his best bet
For any mixed crowd, he'd have reason to fret

But why now Afghanistan, is his concern
For a decade or more, there is no change to learn

What of this big speech, after his summer break
Threatening more allies, not a new mistake

Just how many times, did he blame Obama
Enough finger-pointing, Bush gave us this trauma

With disdain, you repeat, of what you've inherited
How 'bout jobs, the economy, success you've not merited

So bask in a rally, in Arizona
And pardon a sheriff, from Maricopa

Confirm you're a racist, supreme and white
Further proof to this country, for this job, you're not right

LOYALTY TO LUNACY

It's about ego, and how he gets it fed
By his brand, by his tweets, or the lies he has said

Sure he found people's pain, and spoke it out loud
And gave them a loud voice, many now, not so proud

And he seemed legitimate, by his book and show
"What you don't know can hurt you", is what, you should know

He needed minions, and that's what he's found
A way to curry favor, with those not truth bound

Most are good Americans, whom don't like our path
Who's quality of life, has now "taken a bath"

The rich have got richer, the rest "not so much"
Congress in gridlock, apathetic, out of touch

Trump warns of bogeymen, all with a new face
Obama, Susan Rice, or the whole not white race

And Judges of Asian, and Hispanic descent
In his eyes not worthy, they've not paid him rent

He envies knowledge, and legitimacy
Those respected, with accountability

Trump likes dictators, against each human right
Propped up regimes, with net worth out-of-sight

They come to the White House, our democracy
Where Trump can learn from them, kleptocracy

DC lawyers, shun him, won't come to his aid
Not worth the *hit*, to reputations well-made

Won't pay legal bills, or keep his big mouth shut
He won't take advice, or his late night tweets cut

Now obstruction of justice, looks like his new friend
With the bridges he's burned, it's a well-deserved end

THE BUCK STOPS NEAR

Unlike Mr. Truman, Mr. Trump can't abide
That accountable puts, at risk ones own hide

So he cherry picks wins, or in invents them at will
While he blames every loss, on the folks, "On The Hill"

Most that he'll own, is of, invented things
His delusions of winning, and the spin he sings

He's not a great leader, and not a great man
Just a narcissist conman, grabbing limelight he can

He lacks patience and wisdom, and diplomacy
Certainly, he's no statesman, that's easy to see

Perhaps he's a "moron", a la Secretary Rex
Just creating chaos, and a slew of train wrecks

So he'll stress test the country, and find out if it breaks
Not so much a plan, by his trove of mistakes

Now he's just biding time, and offering distraction
While Mueller investigates, to his satisfaction

Then perhaps we'll be done, with this clown of a man
Or the midterms might end him, either sounds like a plan

DON'T ABHOR THE CORE

There're so many Americans, disenfranchised today
They've lost income, great jobs, and here they'll likely stay

With government, representative, of increasingly not them
They're outraged and angry, and quite ready to condemn

When a strong voice they know, leads a rallying cry
It seems a no-brainer, to give that voice a try

Sure their choice is abhorrent, something we all know now
But their reasons quite valid, our support we should vow

They possess no plan, and they trust this voice will
So they'll give up carte blanche, now with all things they're chill

They've no second choice, they've no where else to go
They've bought in completely, so loyalty they'll show

This class has been brewing, for many a year
Politicians missed signs, of a breaking point near

With a Congress ineffective, just lobbyists get served
Reputations are tainted, and no clout is deserved

Who speaks for the people, while their leader lives delusions
At this point we're uncertain, so hope for, good conclusions

There'll be an awakening, of course, not everyone
Know the haters will stay, from Trump good folks will run

A Serious Case of the Clap

First to clap, with head always bobbing
VP Pence, for Trump's always throbbing

Is Trump just his president, or perhaps, more
Sycophants envy, his depth, to adore

So how does he square, Trump's atrocious behavior
Against the teachings, of his personal savior

It makes no sense, unless faith is presumed
Is his motivation, ascendancy assumed

Is he in it to win it, a hack and lapdog
A toady, heel-licker, even after, being flogged

He's tainted and compromised, by his own hand
And not what we need, to lead this great land

PRESIDENTIAL POSTURE

They say for good posture, stand tall with head high
It shows confidence, and strength, others will buy

We know that's just, the physical part
It won't promote trust, with each spewed brain fart

As words really matter, in our great nation
And those who lead us, should show dedication

Your speech should be thoughtful, each line well considered
Not knee jerk, reactive, opportunities frittered

Messaging should be, part of a great whole
Incoherent ramblings, damage our nation's soul

You're trusted to lead us, as our moral bulwark
So step up and own it, from this role don't shirk

Acknowledge this job, is not about you
Toughen your hide, it's worked for a few

Know that you signed up, for public service
'Cause lying and outbursts, make the nation nervous

It's obvious you're no student, of history
So you're doomed to repeat, what the rest of us see

Rithmatic, Riteing, No Reeding

He's good at division, but not the long form
That day he skipped class, and instead studied porn

Though he's really smart, says his U Penn degree
And if you'd doubt that sheepskin, you're in good company

His addition gets questioned, all totals sky high
His math can't be checked, so don't even try

Subtract he can't do, when it comes to his money
As payments get lost, with mail acting funny

But he can multiply, a mole hill to a mountain
And turn a small slight, to a grand insult fountain

So what about reading, he doesn't partake
That's old news to everyone, and certainly not fake

He writes almost nothing, except for his name
Not even his books, on you Donald, shame

"I've the best memory", he says, "maybe ever"
We conclude he's no genius, but he is, con-man clever

MOORE IS LESS

Concurrently now, you can get Moore and less
This grown man dated children, to which they attest

He'll claim le-gal-ity, down to age sixteen
Always, asked permission, a real parents' dream

So if Roy's at your door, young girls, now hide
Likely not there for 'BAMA, or seeking a bride

And those fifteen or younger, he can't remember
He won't refute it, but implies he was tender

SUCKLING MOTHER RUSSIA

When Trump looks into Putin's eyes
Asks about meddling, which Vlad denies
Trump says, "He means it!"

There're multiple angles, you can ascribe
None of them end, with a big surprise
We've all gleaned it

The first is that Trump, is a sycophant
From strong men approval, is his rant
You can't wean it

His ego needs stroking, his only goal
Seeks acceptance from leaders, with real control
Low esteem it

But most likely the answer, as he doubles down
Compromised by Russians, that are all around
Someone's seen it

So despite Intelligence, from each agency
He acts like a traitor, that makes us less free
Lets all scream it

Sharing a Corner with Moore

Trump's in a corner, another of his making
But this time quite oddly, little interest he's taking

He's over a barrel, few words on Roy Moore
As sexual abuser, Trump's there as before

Just one tweet posted, from King condemnation
Does he now understand, Senate seat confirmation

Though he'll jump on Al Franken, and declare, SAD or BAD
But to any Republican, second chances, be had

HYPOCRITES LOATHE

To our GOP Congress, first do no harm
As the tax bill your foisting, gives up the farm

You have little interest, in our middle class
Except to steal from them, with fake bills you pass

It's clear you're delivering, a suicide pill
Now embracing Trump, you'll soon lose The Hill

So you'll skim revenues, for years to come
Stick Dems with the deficits, hope voters stay dumb

So one and a half trillion, is what, you'll steal away
And crush social programs, for those who can't pay

You'll shame office and self, benefiting a few
When you lose your seat, who'll be there to help you

Foxes Aren't Friends

Of partisan politics, I've had quite enough
The polarization, is ugly and rough

The right and the left, need to move back to center
And in civil discourse, we must all reenter

"You can have your opinions, but not your own facts"**
And where science is solid, we need, stop attacks

Let's call out each schemer, shill, and liar
They don't represent us, from their jobs, let's fire

Our house gets divided, and the country gets weak
One Percenters, big business, get what they seek

We are left with the check, and not a lot more
As they pilfer The Treasury, our greatest horror

Let's not be distracted, by hot button issues
Stop reacting on cue, clear thought, I now wish you

Believe no pronouncements, from our corrupt leaders
As they've put country second, these bottom feeders

Foxes, in the hen house, so you better take notice
All is made possible, by the lead fox, call POTUS

**Senator Daniel Patrick Moynahan
"You are entitled to your opinion. But you are not entitled to your own facts."

Take the Money and Stay

It used to be, to succeed in this land
You built a business, then get cash in hand

But of the most wealthy, of GOP donors
They'd like to skip that step, regardless of groaners

As Republican leaders, get ready to give
As a trillion plus dollars, leaks through their sieve

But this money's not lost, or is the reason
If you're of the richest, it's receiving season

We haven't the funds, that they now seek to gift
This long-term commitment, will cause a huge rift

Beyond self-enrichment, there's a second appeal
In its wake there's cost cutting, so here's the reveal

Deficits from tax breaks, can only be cured
With Social Security, and Medicare, skewered

So they'll get their cake, and yes eat it too
"Damn the will of the people," say unconscionable few

In Name Only

Representative government, that phrase now tainted
Some say it's still true, but with fine brush it's painted

Hijacked, by McConnell's G.O.P.
Looks, reads, and feels wrong, indubitably

We expect that House members, would fall into line
Their tenure's precarious, their terms short on time

But of G.O.P. Senators, they should be ashamed
Rolled over for leadership, and shown they're now tamed

It's a quite slippery slope, failing voters, for donors
Then selling this giveaway, as if they've hit homers

Place a trillion plus deficit, on the, middle class
Do you think we won't notice, and give you a pass

The deceit and the treachery, connived in this bill
That steals from OUR Treasury, then rich pockets fill

Keep "Carryover Interest", and no real reform
Trump scores several million, is this our new norm

For Murkowski and Collins, and Corker, and Flake
Choosing party over country, your commitment rings fake

What of "Regular Order", Maverick John McCain
Your great recent floor speech, washed away, leaving pain

Fiscal conservatives, where is their strident voice
Given a teat to suckle, they now too, made their choice

If it's not about treason, then is it about greed
Why else in the world, would honor, you cede

You've abandoned the electorate, and gone off on your own
Our forefathers would tell you, time to quit, and go home

End of Days of Nightmarish Ways

I know, of a *man-child*, tells so many lies
Has a preference to hear them, no big surprise

He watches a network, with an audience of one
Gifting him memes, on agendas to run

He's aware that down deep, facts won't prove him out
So he'll change the subject, then posture and shout

He knows what's in store, since he's been there before
So like always, he'll press on, till he's shown the door

He's learned to appeal, to how so many feel
What he offers the public, is more steal, than deal

He changes alliances, like most men change shorts
Demands total loyalty, or he extorts

Is it rules or reflexes, in his life he employs
One thing is certain, relations, he destroys

He's convinced he's the best, and not shy in saying
No one else matters, just his name, needs displaying

LIFECYCLE OF DECEPTION

Around the world, we fight the good fight
We're clever, ruthless, and bring lots of might

But in our nation's capital, let's preserve some decorum
So much so in fact, proceedings give boredom

But that's not how it is, when you turn on TV
As Trump gets his dogma, from Sean Hannity

And G.O.P. members, spout talking points later
In harsh diatribes, you'd hear from a hater

Accusations, innuendo, and old-fashioned smear
It's the basis of most, of what you'll likely hear

We've a system that's broken, as we have no statesmen
But powerful lobbies, special-interests create them

They're not here for fairness, or to even appeal
They're shameless in spending, to buy their best deal

This latest tax bill, should highlight their clout
By what Congress and Trump, forgot to take out

Not including, what's added, while no one was looking
This type of conduct, is first class "crook-ing"

An inflection point's needed, where we break this trend
From bought and paid government, we need to mend

It seems Trump's the icon, of what's too extreme
And should he not destroy us, we'll revert to the mean

Valentine Trump: "Stupid Cupid"

First Valentine's Day, in the age of Trump
Will you go grab a pussy, or bitch slap a rump

Will you lie about net worth, to get a girl wet
And promised her riches, which she'll never get

Perhaps wine and dine her, at K.F.C.
Entice her with prenup, by your notary

Try and tell her, hand size, has no relation
Before she walks, on a permanent vacation

Clearly, you got no game, and you're just pretending
You'll see now, your chances, are quickly ending

Perhaps be a gentleman, treat her with respect
As emulating Trump, is a romance train wreck

So instead bring some flowers, card, candy, and wine
As that's how its done, by a loving, Valentine

Always 1st, In the 3rd Person

I'm no therapist, don't play one, on TV
Though I know if you're nuts, with no Ph.D

I'm no lie detector, don't polygraph, for a living
Though I know, not trustworthy, when lies are given

I'm no psychologist, haven't studied, maladjusted
Though I know, a narcissist, when your brain's rusted

To cement the prior, no presidents, are "worse than"
When they've spoke of themselves, referenced in the third person

I'm no, Walter Reed M.D., doing POTUS's physical
Though no, psych exam, which we now deem critical

Tangled Web of Shit

First Cotton and Purdue, combined can't recall
That they ever heard "shit hole", mentioned at all

And then days later, with tandem recollection
They're sure what was *not* said, by psychic connection

A lesson dear Senators, on how memory works
Recalling what *wasn't*, is plainly berserk

The truth will come out, and you two should've owned it
As one more revision, means three times you've blown it

And you've reached this epiphany, mutually
In the annals of science, revolutionary

You can't prove your negative, you both should know
Your misguided loyalty, wins your own shit show

Hush Money Honey

One Hundred, thirty thousand, Stormy earned to stay quiet
Who knows the cost of, Melania's riot

Is she mum on his prowess, or about having sex
Or small hands versus manhood, not rivaling T-Rex

Is he that bad a lover, to pay such a sum
Or was it hazard pay, so she'd stay till he's done

Or perhaps, she's that good, I've not seen her work
Did she praise him, do handstands, and concurrently twerk

Was there a gag order, I don't mean N.D.A.
Throat noise, he demanded, like when big boys play

So porn stars line up, you know what this means
College loans, you can trade, for some nightmarish dreams

MR. WORST ENEMY

Is he itch or twitch, our Commander-in-Chief
One thing's for sure, he loves him, some good grief

We know this is true, because every day
He makes a fresh pot, so his name, we'll say

He believes in that adage of Hollywood
"There's no bad publicity, it's all good"*

That gets his itch scratched, on a daily basis
For one earth rotation, keeps his twitch in stasis

He can't conceive things, were great without him
So he talks things down, that's his narcissism

Perhaps has a variant, of Napoleon Complex
But taller, still damaged, does things by reflex

So Prez wash your mouth out, with a bar of soap
As each word leads you, toward the end of your rope

It's not if, but when, that the end you'll soon see
Point, your finger inward, Mr. Worst Enemy

*There is not a definite attribution available, and the quotation has different adaptations. The earliest inspiration for this is thought to be Oscar Wilde's.

"The only thing worse than being talked about, is not being talked about."

AND WITH A STRAIGHT FACE

Huckabee-Sanders, with her dizzying spin
It requires Bonnie™, just to, listen in

She's matter-of-fact, of all she does say
It lends her speech credence, but those whom know say, "Nay"

Liberties, she takes, pulling things from thin air
As she dodges and weaves, with nary a care

Rode in on Dad's coattails, used nepotism freely
Her knack for misstating, equally unsavory

With facts incomplete, for an *audience of one*
She swings for the fences, to hit Trump a home run

Always talks of the Dems, and how they're to blame
How they'll hurt America, on you Sarah, shame

It's bizarre that she also, speaks for Jeff Flake
And divines his meaning, as attention, That's Fake

You've got some momentum, and wind at your back
But know in the future, you'll be titled a hack

You insult the nation, with your fake news awards
Does the *real* press despise you, just feigning accord

Your words can't be trusted, neither your intentions
And your podium smugness, highlights your pretensions

DREAMS DON'T COME EASY HERE

If DACA is right, then pass it tonight
Because anything else, is just cruel

With good lives insecure, take action so pure
Act in accordance with, "The Golden Rule"

Put agendas aside, let this clean bill ride
Leveraging it, the act of a fool

We know *Dreamers* you broke, and on it you risk choke
Then your legacy, shows you, as a ghoul

So make this a win, before midterms begin
Claiming, you took SAD Congress, to school

Win Big, Lose Bigger

You care about no one, and have no shame
With lies, your norm, your strong suit is blame

You're the most important, in your universe
And good reputations, you need trample and curse

You monopolize attention, as that's what you do
Get outrageous, sensational, puts eyeballs on you

To those well-liked, you form strong opposition
And in doing so, take a contrary position

For a shrinking minority, you're their special guy
But as they know you better, they'll wonder why

As your veil is lowered, you'll be seen as you are
Good people won't tolerate, a cheat and a liar

Your legal troubles, will then quickly balloon
And with those you held sway, they'll abandon you soon

Only money and lawyers, will stay by your side
Yet those will recede, like an ebbing tide

No one left to sell to, no one left to con
You'll realize, your undoing, began when you won

DECEPTION'S DARK PRINCE

Like folks from Wisconsin, I trust Paul Ryan
To *not* tell the truth, and smugly keep lying

He's aligned himself, with the uber rich
Paid for his service, scratching their every itch

Some say it's murder, that he's committing
Killing social programs, Tax Cuts now permitting

He's the worst of the Congress, lacks morality
Representative, is what, he can't seem to be

You can see when he speaks, he tries to look serious
Though he's hiding a smirk, that leaves people furious

It's looking quite likely, this is his last term
With one big bill passed, contributions he'll earn

Perhaps he'll try his hand, in the private sector
Likely a lobbyist, public trust's not a factor

IIe's helped dent America, hopcfully not brokcn
Cashing in his chips, gave our Treasury a soaking

"Good riddance to bad rubbish", is what the Brits say
And with his, approval numbers, he'll be on his away

Higher Expectations and Better Relations

To expect more, you might think, is our naïveté
We demand a fair process, it's our democratic way

We're no fans of the stunts, by McConnell and Ryan
Employing duplicity, deception, and lyin'

To win at all costs, drops the bar out of sight
And invites, next in power, to one-up each slight

Bipartisan, is of which, they're vaguely aware
But they've proved with frequency, for it they don't care

They've not represented, nor legislated
They've just served their donors, and our process, berated

They've cast out the notion, of what is fair play
They write bills on Monday, call votes on Tuesday

Blocked hearings on a, High Court nominee
Their temerity is staining, our history

Then they'll quote Obama, to support their spin
And in their next breath, doubt he's, American

Though they're just a symptom, the problem's with few
It's lobbyists for Fat Cats, who's bidding they do

We've a Congress, by name, until we secure
Independent Representatives, of who's motives, we're sure

A Ful Year

It's been a year, and we're still here
For that we should be grateful

Each Trump surprise, risks our demise
Toward many he's so hateful

With *Rocketman*, who's nukes that can
Reach us in ways so fateful

Each Russian plot, which he sees not
And still we have a plateful

It makes us SAD, that he's so BAD
This President, most distasteful

Never Trump! Forever Trump.
Whatever, Trump?

Among real Republicans, there's great disbelief
Even recent Never-Trumpers, stopped gritting their teeth

It's caused consternation, to G.O.P. faithful
Adding to their quandary, they find it distasteful

"It happened so fast", is so often said
Did the dogma change, since I went to bed

I'd offer their premise, isn't booked for arrival
As it ain't policy, but political survival

With a fox in the hen house, even roosters are scared
Once he took residence, just the loyal are spared

Trump's taught establishment, what candidates learned
That the rules and norms, are easily spurned

So with no understanding, how to escape his wrath
They chose self-preservation, and followed his path

These folks are quite flexible, and go with the flow
Having got to this level, this much they all know

There're are few acts of bravery, not of a swan song
As the system will whack you, like when moles stand strong

For Congressman, Senators, or each sycophant
If they've made a 180, then for Trump they now rant

As most were raised, in an age of compliance
Relinquishing backbones, while pledging alliance

So when leaders saw Trump, as their ticket to ride
They rallied the troops, and now they too abide

Yet when Trump self-destructs, they'll again realign
And like lemmings they'll follow, s/he whom leads the line

NICKNAME FOR SHAME

Congratulations, Representative Schiff
Trump gave you a nickname, while in a tiff

It's a badge of honor, that you should wear well
As he names those that threaten, in hopes to dispel

Perhaps he was being, the most presidential
And thereby confirming, he's run out of potential

Cares not for dissenters, or those with no love
As in all things he's great, from his pedestal above

He attracts the worst elements, into his sphere
As they speak the same language, this much is now clear

For if he truly liked you, you'd be under suspicion
Though you'll never be his guy, your most solid position

STATE OF THE UMION

"The State of The Union," is a time honored phrase
Yet it's not indicative, of our current ways

You see the word "Union", infers all inclusive
Where our President favors, rich and exclusive

So describe which Union, his speech will address
While folks are uneasy, as he foments unrest

Does what he says matter, this purveyor of lies
Runs a criminal enterprise, in front of our eyes

He undermines others, working on his behalf
Demands oaths of loyalty, ain't that a laugh

But to whom is he loyal, the question's rhetorical
As the answer, just him, requires no oracle

His bar is set low, if he'll follow the script
And read what's written, while not saying "shit"

He could sound presidential, he's done it before
Tomorrow's tweets will show, its him, nothing more

Maybe from the hip quips, like each morning tweet
Will gin up his base, and turn up the heat

He'll give his big speech, perhaps his one and only
So listen, but consider, this guy's one big phony

PLEADING LEAVES ALL NEEDING

Donald Trump is our test, and a world-class mess
Of democracy's, ideals today

He's rejected all norms, yet his tax return forms
Will tell us, how much did he pay

He creates so much drama, still rails on Obama
Still talks, of locking Hillary, away

While sycophant Nunes, steals away to Trump, soon as
His committee members, look astray

There's a hunt for Bob Mueller, though he remains cooler
Than an igloo, on a winter's day

And the lawyers hire lawyers, while a Wolff sits in foyers
As Bannon shows, edges now fray

We've a porn star in tow, money moves to and fro
Is it laundered, or hush, they'll not say

They don't need rule of law, it gets stuck in their craw
As it stops them, from having their way

Trump's laryngitis, in Constitutional Crisis
"Pleads the Fifth", his smartest play

COMMANDER-SANS-GRIEF

Another mass shooting, and still Trump's, unprepared
An accident of birth, from empathy, he's spared

When it comes to emotions, he is damaged goods
And as well apathetic, he cares not when he should

So one more trip to Florida, to his private club
And close by Parkland murders, he can't fully snub

So he visits the area, for photo ops
And smiles, with thumbs up, with Docs and Cops

And says he won't golf, out of respect
But that didn't last long, as you would expect

So on Presidents' Day, funerals began
He did not attend, but had putter in hand

He's a horrible person, and so he won't atone
You'd have better luck squeezing, blood from a stone

HOPE HICKS FINAL FIX

Is Hope Hicks, the hottest of chics
Chose by Trump, in our White House today

At a mere, 29, with looks so divine
Made *Director*, though with little to say

And she's rarely heard, and that seems absurd
As Communications, are her mainstay

When it comes to Trump, she's there at each stump
Fawning in, the most dutiful way

With Porter now gone, will Trump come on strong
And to whom then, will she run away

Bob Mueller's a choice, and by speaking her voice
She'll walk free, with no one to obey

Or perhaps she'll hang in, take it on the chin
And with pardon, she'll get a stay

Though she'll carry the stain, and with it the shame
Knowing the price, was too high to pay

But if Rob is her guy, we'll see her with black eye
Ending this tale, so *Whack* and *Cray-Cray*

Wait, there's still more, Hope walked out the door
While we all thought, she had feet of clay

Perhaps with her beau gone, she just can't carry on
She's the latest rat, to leave the fray

COHEN OF SILENCE

"Oh no you did-n't", might say, Michael Cohen
As the FBI raided, his hotel home

And also his office, and home renovation
Clearly he's feeling, this conflagration

Muller referred it, to Rod Rosenstein
As NY's Southern District, fell into line

So the Justice Department, showed they were all in
And that set the stage, for the raids to begin

It wasn't a "break-in", as Trump has opined
But a well vetted op, simultaneously timed

And what Trump calls, "Witch Hunt", is "Rule of Law"
And "bad for the country", is his old, tired saw

So we'll wait a few days, as the Feds sort it all
And watch Trump convulse, as he fears, Cohen's fall

Like a legal piñata, taking too many whacks
It's now Cohen's turn, to suffer attacks

Has the bullet been fired, Cohen will take for Trump
If hyperbole, Cohen won't be, Trump's latest chump

LAW OF LARGE BLUNDERS

Unintended consequences, will be unforeseen
And often they're triggered, from things not mainstream

With a constant barrage, from one whom flings feces
He acts from slights, that now, only he sees

There's no strategizing, no wonk in his tweets
He just shoots from the lip, past K.F.C. eats

His singular dogma, is to make people twitch
And to watch them in vain, trying to scratch his itch

He's victim and bully, through a binary voice
Though plays as uniter, a most short-lived choice

At times there'll be outcomes, favorable
Of his methods, outliers, state nothing at all

With discipline lacking, and no plan in site
Even Fox and Friends can't, contain their fright

Blind squirrels and Broke Clocks, succeed everyday
Let's examine causality, before we praise, his way

The New Smell of Success

If you have no shame, score one point in this game
And score two, if pretending you do

If you never feel guilt, then this game will tilt
In your favor, points accrue, to you

Can't share sympathy, or know what that'd be
Then kindness, you need not eschew

No concern for others, or their personal druthers
Then you'll never be stymied, or blue

With no moral compass, won't be vexed by the rumpus
That compassionate, people, suffer through

So congrats you're just fine, in this Trumpian time
As you have "IT", much like shit, on a shoe

Do Your Other Best

The ABA, has now taken pause
On Judge Cavanagh's, greatest flaws

As per Justice Stevens, it's his slant
But for many it's his, unbridled rant

His entitlement, unabashedly shows
As he states, "Yale Law", his horn he blows

Perhaps temperament, is his greatest failing
And inso his support, is quickly curtailing

Disrespecting the Senators, who questioned him
Shows a demeanor, that's deep within

The FBI inquiry, around Dr. Ford
Not "cover-worthy", shield it won't afford

So "impartial" is something, we'll likely not see
Nor is "independent", where he'll likely be

Senators show us, a higher ideal
Quash this nomination, with it's process surreal

So with norms out the window, the High Court you will stain
If you offer *Consent*, as this man will bring shame

A Boy and A Diary

He records kids names, that meet after school
And swears that he lives, by the Golden Rule

But for someone so conscious, of his own behavior
Not recording attacks, is his choice in his favor

No mention he fancies, even one gal
Confirming each female, is strictly a pal

Has no girlfriend, but each night talks to girls
Yet shares more attraction, for guys, squats, and curls

Do his hormones rage, for the boys on his teams
Is it tight ends that star, in all his wet dreams

"Works his tail off", he'll repeatedly say
Is his the behavior, of a closeted gay

It would explain Lindsey's, impassioned appeal
As brother-to-brother, is how they best feel

That alleged attack, seems something he'd do
If gay and goaded, by a buddy or two

He's the worst of elite, clumsy and unsure
But feels most entitled, in his drunken blur

And beer equals courage, but it's much more than that
Letting his alter ego, step up and bat

He really likes brewskis, he proudly exclaims
Was he drunk and belligerent, to enjoy gang bangs

As a captain of teams, he never got laid
At least by a girl, is the angle he played

This overachiever, may be wrapped too tight
And to parental pressures, he can't push back or fight

So he stays in the lanes, where he'll be well accepted
And attacks unknown girls, so he won't risk, rejected

Now he cries like a girl, 'cause he's never been tested
On the flipside of judgment, his emotions are bested

So he goes all *Ike Turner*, on those weighing him
Shows temperament unworthy, and rage from within

Is the High Court the place, for a man with such traits
Not forthcoming, and cagey, is where he really rates

ORANGE SOBS OVER MOBS

"We create jobs, and the Dems create mobs"
Easy to remember, for Trump, Rush, and Dobbs

Sure it is catchy, and has a nice ring
But like most of Trump's words, they don't mean a thing

The jobs being created, are of Obama's making
Outside the Orange Bubble, none are mistaking

Mobs are but "masses", with behavior dependent
Shopper and fan mobs, seek the resplendent

When Trump talks of mobs, he must think of each rally
Riotous and inciting, like in a back alley

Americans formed mobs, under British rule
And at the Bastille, French mobs were *tres* cool

Mobs, are the option, for the unrepresented
When monarchs and despots, don't feel complimented

Mobs form of those suffering, lies or slights
As when you betray them, mobs fight for their rights

So yes Mr. President, you'll reap what you sow
As a Nationalist, White Supremacist, your mobs too, now grow

FINAL ACT ABOUT FACT

The ides of November, will mark the time
When Trump shirked his first Love, that light, so lime

He's feeling the pressure, and with it the fear
His congressional cover, it's end being near

In forty-five days, "45" will be through
In being unchecked, as he's become, used to

His hand now is weak, with acting AG
At best, Hail Mary, all can clearly see

So he pouts, throws tantrums, seeks someone to blame
He will lie-taunt-demean, with his flickering flame

He knows that his family, will soon be indicted
Still he tries bullying Mueller, while claiming he's slighted

So he'll be more erratic, yes there is still room
A chaos agent, like a red algae bloom

So he'll sit in his bedroom, with the walls closing in
And watch "Fox News", and bathe in it's din

Though it's not in his nature, to just fade away
Perhaps with comeuppance, he'll choose not to stay

'Cause if he sticks around, it will hit the wall
Know he'll blow up the country, rather than take his fall

TRUMP SCROOGES HIMSELF

The asylum now, is run by inmates
As Trump's last two generals, have sealed fates

White House Chief of Staff, General Kelly
Fired by text, by Trump's spine of jelly

And General Mattis, the D.O.D.'s
Quits in protest, when Syria, Trump flees

The three months notice, that Mattis provided
Trump cut to weeks, and inso derided

So by year's end, more adults leave the room
Now wackos and weirdos, alone will then loom

While all replacements, crawl from the swamp
Unqualified, biased, installed they'll soon romp

The new ones are temps, as few will step up
And those that Trump chooses, just won't say, "yup!"

Sans Defense, Interior, and an AG
Cabinet postings, are now minus three

It's business as usual, of his own creation
So this New Year, brings Dems, and more, investigations

HE QUACKS LIKE

Let's pull the lens back, and get some clarity
Turn down the noise, and see what we see

Then review all his actions, since his nomination
Then conclude they're part, of Kremlin's domination

We can start with some planks, in the R's platform
Which did not require, so much as a quorum

Still won't acknowledge, the election hacks
As Putin was firm, denying attacks

Then division with, our Western allies
Talks breaking up NATO, no big surprise

Has no use for courts, or the F.B.I.
And he'll work to end them, or at least he'll try

He wouldn't use sanctions, till Congress voted
Then dragged his feet, till he even noted

But he loves each dictator, and strong man
Russian, Turkish, Saudi, and North Korean

His cabinet, an embarrassment, with revolving door
Financial malfeasance, en masse, what a horror

Can't grasp why The Fed, won't do his bidding
Speaks of obstruction, then says he was kidding

Withdrawals from Syria, he now telegraphs
One more win for Putin, earns belly laughs

An excellent reason, to keep taxes from view
The Russian State issue, of his W-2

WRITHING ON HIS WALL

Nancy Pelosi, whom the "R's" love to hate
Served Trump, humble pie, on a king size plate

His shutdown, a la mode, his latest extortion
Not since bankruptcy court, has he had such a portion

The first clue, that his royal reign, has now ceased
As the Democrats' power, in The House, has increased

And his days of dictating, unilaterally
Are now by the wayside, not tragically

So like other bullies, when you called their bluff
They get quiet, compliant, and don't act so tough

As they know now, their leverage, has evaporated
With no new alliances, their future's ill-fated

So stuck between Nancy, Ann, and his base
The look of his end game, is etched in his face

CLOTHESHORSE IN ORANGE

Roger Stone, is no longer, alone
Now indicted, with all of his peeps

Gates and Manafort, might see him in court
As Mueller, is playing for keeps

His charade, almost through, and the grandstanding too
As reality, in his brain, seeps

No more cavalier, of WikiLeaks here
To grand juries now, he'll disclose, heaps

Facing long prison time, you won't have to remind
What once sowed, now, he reaps

Goodbye, bespoke clothes, for jumpsuits, with your Bro's
It's your fault, your tailor, now weeps

So now, flip like a rat, on your back, get a pat
Showing you're, the king of, Trump's creeps

RAIDER AND TRAITOR

Benedict Arnold, gets a run for his money
And if Mudd is your surname, your future's less cruddy

The contender has now, established his *cred*
It's that Orange haired guy, looking more, Russian Red

He's against institutions, not loyal to him
And with our country's friends, there's no "thick or thin"

He's not a big reader, just shares what he's told
As his reign, oops "term", now starts to unfold

Of his vast wrong doings, they're lifting the veil
Collusion, witness tampering, extramarital tail

There's tax evasion, and Campaign violation
Transition Team deals, and his crooked Foundation

With so many questions, on the, Inauguration
Still a fraction of those, of his Organization

Its clear, greed and ego, are the binary reason
He's an odds-on-favorite, to be charged, with High Treason

www.ingramcontent.com/pod-product-compliance
Lightning Source LLC
Chambersburg PA
CBHW060356290526
45791CB00002B/533